United States
Department of
Agriculture

Forest Service

**Southern
Research Station**

e-Resource Bulletin
SRS–170

Forest Resources on Mississippi's National Forests, 2006

Sonja N. Oswalt

The Author:

Sonja N. Oswalt, Forester, U.S. Forest Service,
Southern Research Station, Knoxville, TN 37919.

Cover photo:

Sign on the Chickasaw off highway vehicle trail on the Tombibbee National Forest in
Mississippi. (photo by Sonja Oswalt, U.S. Department of Agriculture Forest Service)

April 2011

Southern Research Station
200 W.T. Weaver Blvd.
Asheville, NC 28804

Contents

[a] All tables in this report are available in Microsoft® Excel workbook files. Upon request, these files will be supplied in the format the customer requests. The use of trade or firm names in this publication is for reader information and does not imply endorsement by the U.S. Department of Agriculture of any product or service.

Forest Resources of Mississippi's National Forests, 2006

Sonja N. Oswalt

Abstract

This bulletin describes forest resource characteristics of Mississippi's national forests, with emphasis on DeSoto National Forest, following the 2006 survey completed by the U.S. Department of Agriculture Forest Service, Forest Inventory and Analysis program. Mississippi's national forests comprise >1 million acres of forest land (about 7 percent of all forest land in the State) and contain nearly 11 percent of the State's standing live-tree biomass. National forests in Mississippi are dominated by softwood species, including ecologically important longleaf pine ecosystems. Compared with other public as well as private forests in the State, Mississippi's national forests are older, contain bigger trees, experience fewer removals but higher mortality levels, and contain a larger number of standing dead trees.

Keywords: DeSoto National Forest, FIA, forest inventory, Mississippi, Mississippi national forests.

Introduction

Mississippi's National Forest System (NFS) comprises six national forests and seven ranger districts across the State. The six forests that makeup the system include Bienville National Forest, Homochitto National Forest, Delta National Forest, Holly Springs National Forest, Tombigbee National Forest, and DeSoto National Forest (fig. 1). These forests offer multiple-use opportunities to Mississippi's residents and visitors, and provide the ongoing renewable ecosystem services of clean water, timber, and wildlife and fish habitat.

DeSoto National Forest is the largest of Mississippi's six national forests and contains Mississippi's only national scenic river. Additionally, the forest contains a large proportion of the State's longleaf pine resources—an ecologically valuable ecosystem that is home to multiple rare wildlife species. DeSoto National Forest is located in the South Forest Inventory and Analysis (FIA) unit of Mississippi, and was the national forest most heavily impacted by Hurricane Katrina, which made landfall in 2005.

The FIA program of the U.S. Department of Agriculture Forest Service is tasked with measuring and reporting on forest resources on public and private land across the United States. In 2006, sampling on Mississippi's national forests consisted of 229 plots across all forests, or about one plot for every 6,000 acres. Future plans for sampling on national forests in Mississippi include intensifying the sample to obtain a larger sample size and lower variability (and thus, statistical error). This report is intended to serve as a baseline for comparison with future data collection and reporting efforts on Mississippi's national forests.

Mississippi's national forests are surrounded by a matrix of private and public land. This report compares the NFS lands in the State with statewide resource data. In addition, this report provides additional comparison data for DeSoto National Forest and surrounding South-unit non-Federal forest land because of DeSoto's prominence as the largest national forest in the State, its unique longleaf pine natural resource, and its distinction as the national forest most heavily impacted by Hurricane Katrina.

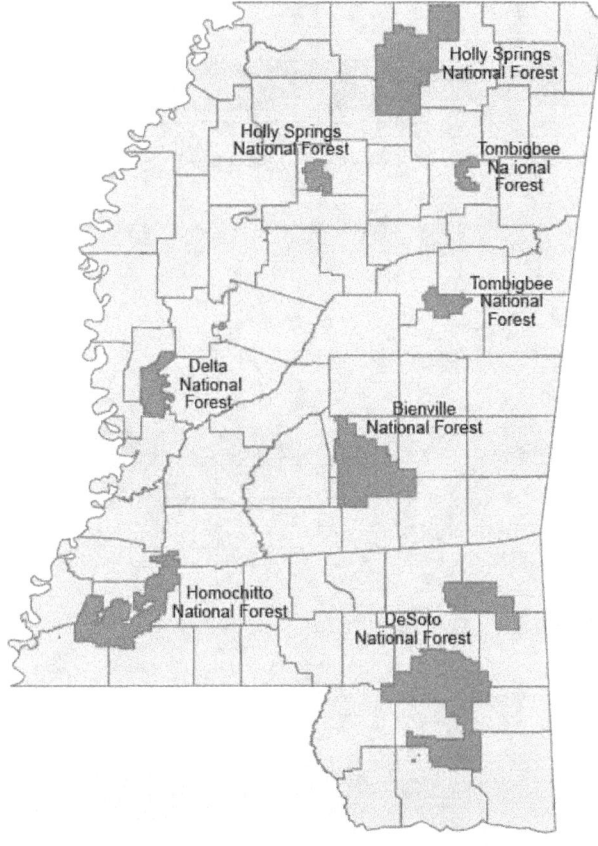

Figure 1—Location of Mississippi's national forests.

Highlights

- The number of live trees per acre on Mississippi's national forests is lower than the number of live trees per acre statewide. This is likely because trees on the national forests tend to be larger in diameter and older than the statewide average.

- Per-acre live-tree biomass is much higher on national forests in Mississippi than the statewide average.

- Per-acre average annual net growth of live trees was lower on national forests than the statewide average, particularly on DeSoto National Forest. DeSoto's net growth likely was affected by the impacts of Hurricane Katrina, which made landfall near DeSoto in 2005.

- Per-acre average annual mortality was higher on national forests, particularly DeSoto National Forest, compared to statewide averages.

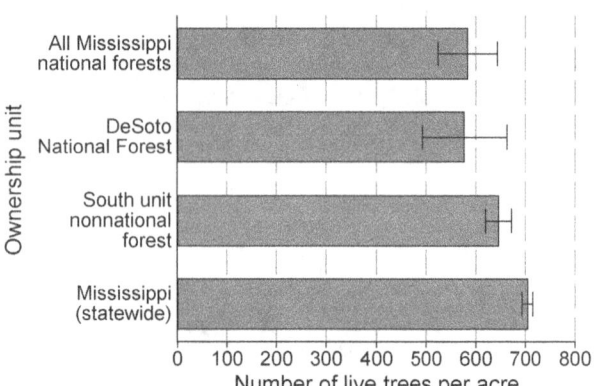

Number of live trees per acre of forest land (± 1 standard error) by ownership unit, Mississippi, 2006.

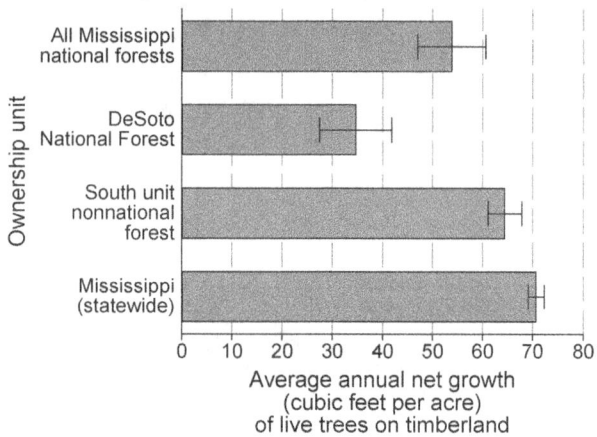

Average annual net growth of live trees per acre of timberland (± 1 standard error) by ownership unit, Mississippi, 2006.

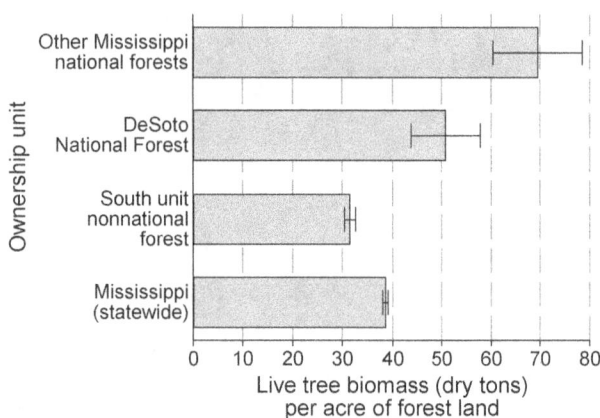

Live-tree biomass per acre of forest land (± 1 standard error) by ownership unit, Mississippi, 2006.

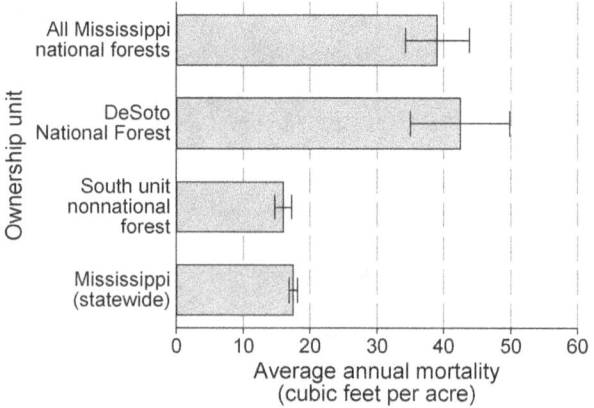

Average annual mortality of live trees on timberland (± 1 standard error) by ownership unit, Mississippi, 2006.

- Per-acre average annual removals on Mississippi's national forests were much lower than statewide averages.

- The per-acre number of live seedlings on national forest forest land was comparable to statewide averages, except DeSoto National Forest, where the number of live seedlings were fewer than statewide averages. In contrast, the per-acre number of live trees > 18 inches diameter at breast height (d.b.h.) was higher on national forests and DeSoto National Forest than statewide averages.

- The per-acre number of standing dead trees (snags) on national forest forest land was higher than statewide averages.

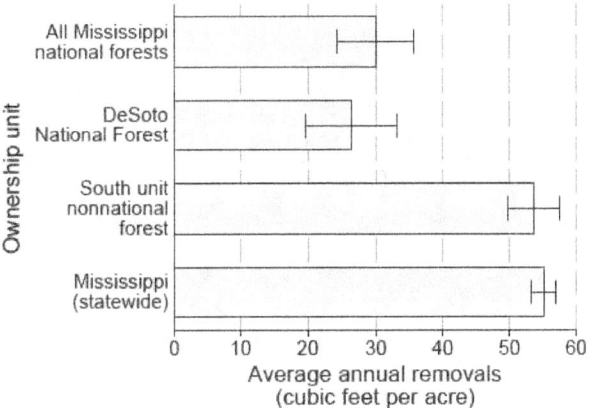

Average annual removals timberland (± 1 standard error) by ownership unit, Mississippi, 2006.

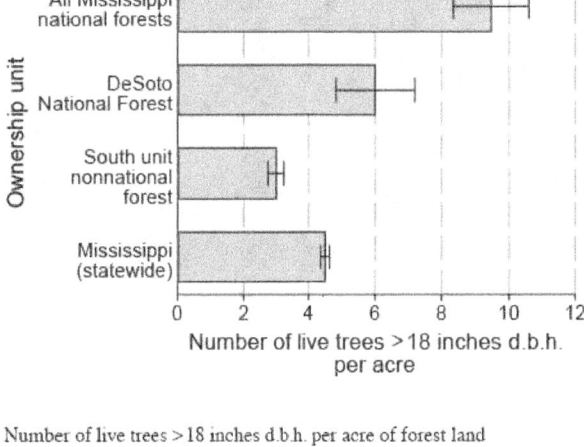

Number of live trees > 18 inches d.b.h. per acre of forest land (± 1 standard error) by ownership unit, Mississippi, 2006.

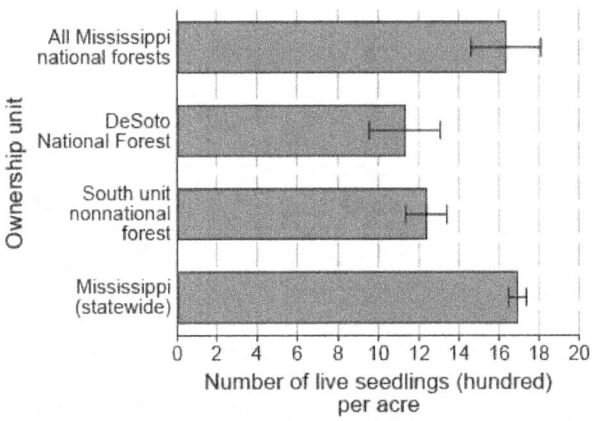

Number of live seedlings per acre of forest land (± 1 standard error) by ownership unit, Mississippi, 2006.

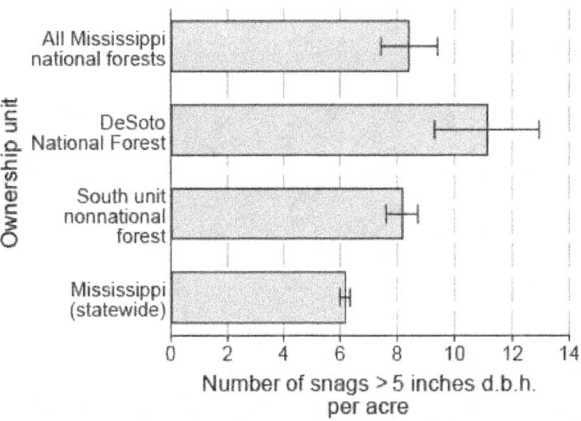

Number of standing dead trees (snags) > 5 inches d.b.h. per acre of forest land (± 1 standard error) by ownership unit, Mississippi, 2006.

Longleaf pine and wiregrass forest (photo by Bill Lea, U S Department of Agriculture Forest Service)

Forest Land and Timberland Area

- There are > 1 million acres of forest land on national forests in Mississippi. FIA considers 99 percent of that land to be timberland.

- Since 1977, timberland area on national forests has remained stable at 1.3 (± 0.08) million acres.[1]

- National forests in Mississippi account for 7 percent of statewide forest land.

- Fifty-six percent of forest land acreage on national forests in the State is in a softwood forest-type group.

- Loblolly-shortleaf pine is the most common forest-type group on Mississippi's national forest forest land, followed by longleaf-slash pine and oak-hickory.

- Thirty-six percent of forest land on national forests, statewide, is in the loblolly-shortleaf forest-type group (fig. 2).

- Longleaf-slash pine forests occupy 264,043 acres on national forests, statewide (fig. 3). That represents about 35 percent of all longleaf-slash pine acreage in the State.

- Ninety-seven percent of longleaf-slash pine forests on national forests in Mississippi occur on DeSoto National Forest in south Mississippi.

---

[1] Forest and timberland acreage reported by FIA will differ from the acreage reported by the NFS because FIA estimates are generated using a statistical sample, which contains a degree of unavoidable statistical error, while NFS totals are based on land sales and acquisitions as determined by property surveys.

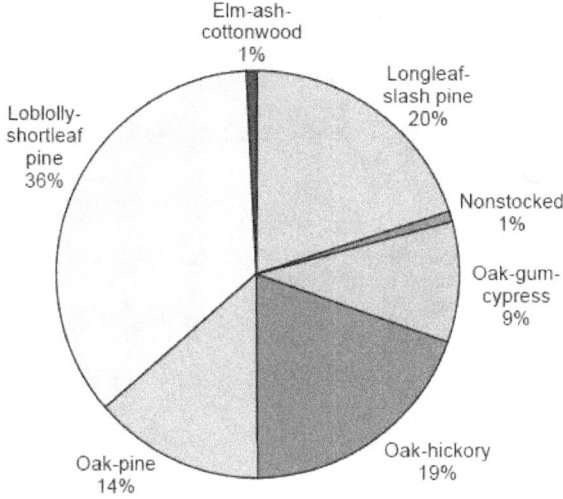

Figure 2—Proportion of national forest forest land by forest-type group, Mississippi, 2006.

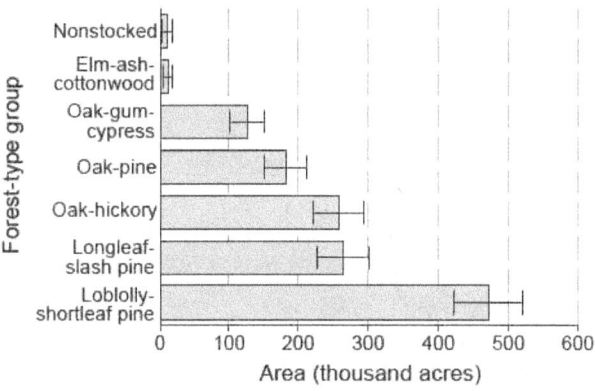

Figure 3—Area of national forest forest land (± 1 standard error) by forest-type group, Mississippi, 2006.

- DeSoto National Forest accounts for 46 percent of Federal forest land in Mississippi, making it an important component of Mississippi's national forest heritage.

National forests in Mississippi encompass a diversity of forest types in a variety of ecological settings. Softwoods occupy the majority of national forest forest land in Mississippi. Even though national forests makeup only 7 percent of the State's forest land area, they support over one-third of the longleaf-slash pine forest land.

Of the national forest forest land area occupied by longleaf-slash pine, most of this land (with longleaf-slash pine) occurs within the boundaries of DeSoto National Forest in the South FIA survey unit. Longleaf pine is a treasured species in the Southern Coastal Plain because it supports a unique, fire-dominated, park-like ecological community that is home to a variety of rare plants, birds, and mammals, including the endangered red-cockaded woodpecker.

Species Composition

- Forest land on the national forests in Mississippi supports 774.2 million live trees, while timberland supports 765.7 million live trees.

- The number of trees per acre on all national forest timberland in Mississippi has decreased from 768 (± 75) trees per acre to 582 (± 59) trees per acre since 1977 (fig. 4).

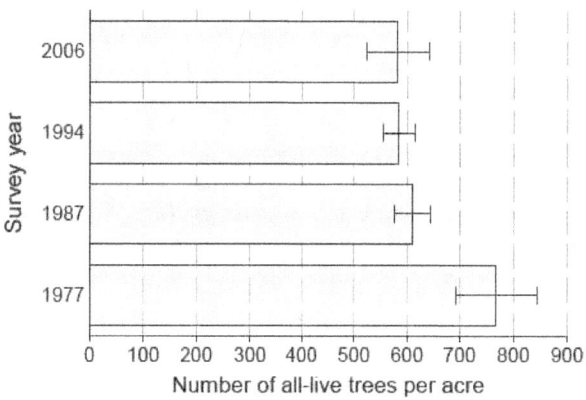

Figure 4—Number of all-live trees per acre on national forest timberland (± 1 standard error) by survey year, Mississippi.

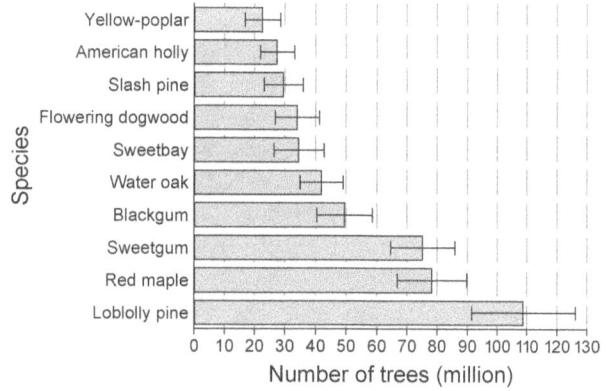

Cypress-Tupelo stand in Mississippi (photo by Bill Lea,
U S Department of Agriculture Forest Service)

- The most common individual species is loblolly pine,
  with 108.9 (± 17.4) million estimated live trees on forest
  land (fig. 5).

- In terms of basal area, the dominant species on
  Mississippi's national forests are loblolly pine, slash pine,
  longleaf pine, white oak, and sweetgum (fig. 6). In terms
  of numbers of live trees, the dominant species are loblolly
  pine, red maple, sweetgum, blackgum, and water oak
  (fig. 5).

- There is an average of 577 trees per acre on DeSoto
  National Forest forest land, as compared to 645 trees per
  acre on non-Federal land surrounding DeSoto National
  Forest, 589 trees per acre on all other national forests in
  Mississippi, and 704 trees per acre, on average, in all of
  Mississippi.

Figure 5—Number of 10 most frequently recorded live-tree species on
national forest forest land (± 1 standard error), Mississippi, 2006.

6

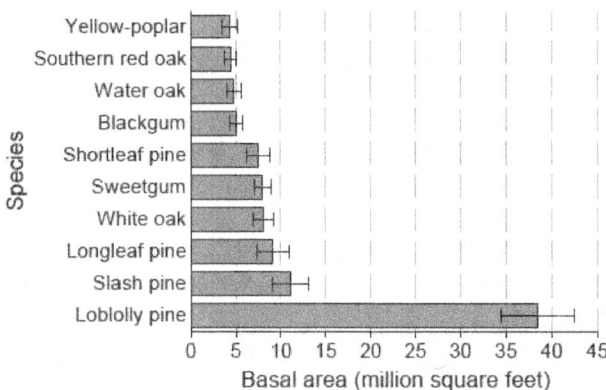

Figure 6—Basal area of top 10 live-tree species on national forest forest land (± 1 standard error), Mississippi, 2006.

Species composition has changed as well. In 1977, the top five most frequently encountered trees on national forest timberland in Mississippi were loblolly pine, blackgum, flowering dogwood, sweetgum, and red maple (fig. 7). In 2006, while loblolly pine was still most common, red maple, sweetgum, blackgum, and water oak were the next most frequently encountered trees (fig. 5). Between 1977 and 2006, flowering dogwood populations on NFS land declined by 63 percent. Flowering dogwood has been undergoing declines throughout its native range because of infestation by dogwood anthracnose (*Discula destructiva*; Holzmueller and others 2006). The known range of dogwood anthracnose does not currently include Mississippi; however, the precipitous decline in dogwood populations on Mississippi's national forests and elsewhere in the State warrants further investigation.

• DeSoto National Forest supports about 351.2 million live trees, the majority (64 percent) of which are hardwood trees < 5.0 inches in diameter.

Mississippi is well known for its lush southern pine forests. The national forests in Mississippi reflect that southern pine heritage with an assemblage of trees dominated by yellow pines. Fast-growing species like red maple and sweetgum occupy the understory of pine and mixed hardwood forests, and spring up in areas that have been previously cleared. In addition to pine forests, national forests in Mississippi extend into another important resource, the bottomland hardwood forest. Supporting beautiful cypress, tupelo, water oak, and other water-tolerant species, bottomland hardwoods are a treasured resource in the State, and are home to unique plant and animal communities.

Since 1977, the number of trees per acre on Mississippi's national forest timberland has decreased by 24 percent (fig. 4). The decline likely is the result of the self-thinning of suppressed trees as dominant and codominant trees grow larger. Thus, while the national forest acreage has remained stable, trees are getting bigger and each individual tree is occupying more space.

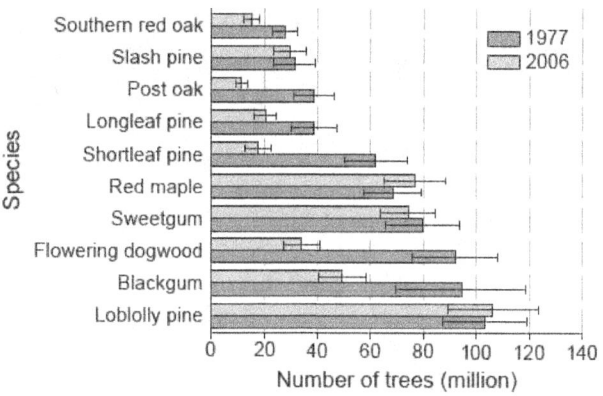

Figure 7—Number of top 10 live-tree species on national forest forest land (± 1 standard error) compared to 2006 populations, Mississippi.

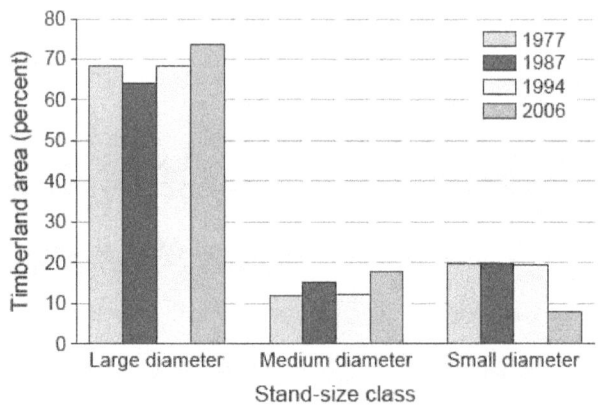

Prescribed fire on DeSoto National Forest, Mississippi (photo by Jay Boykin, U S Department of Agriculture Forest Service)

Stand Size and Age

- Seventy-three percent of timberland on Mississippi national forests is classified as large diameter, up from 68 percent of timberland in 1977 and 1994. In contrast, only 8 percent of timberland is classified as small diameter, down from 20 percent in 1977 and 19 percent in 1994 (fig. 8).

- The area of timberland classified as large diameter on DeSoto National Forest has increased 11 percent from 58 percent in 1994 to 69 percent in 2006, while small diameter timberland area has decreased from 20 percent to 9 percent, a difference of 11 percent.

- Statewide across all ownerships, for comparison, 46 percent of forest land is classified as large diameter, while 27 percent is classified as small diameter.

- On Mississippi's national forests, 60 percent of timberland is > 50 years old, and only 16 percent is < 20 years old. In comparison, 78 percent of timberland across all ownerships statewide is < 50 years old, and 43 percent is < 20 years old.

Figure 8—Proportion of national forest timberland area by stand-size class and survey year, Mississippi.

8

Trees on national forests in Mississippi are, on average, older than trees in the rest of the State. Aging forests on national forests are becoming a common trend as land management goals and priorities have changed toward more ecological and aesthetic values and away from commodity production. While old trees can be a good thing, a preponderance of aging trees can mean a loss of habitat for early-successional wildlife species, a decline in forest health as trees begin to senesce and become more susceptible to insects and disease, and an eventual change in composition or eventual decline in large, old trees as turnover occurs. However, if forest land on the surrounding landscape supports primarily young forests, national forests can offer refuge for wildlife that require large, mature trees to reproduce and survive.

One way to provide early-successional habitat for wildlife species in maturing forests is through canopy gaps or local disturbances that may be too patchy for FIA data to adequately capture on the landscape. Hurricane Katrina pummeled the Gulf Coast in August 2005, bringing with it hurricane-force winds, massive rainfall, and related tornado damage that extended throughout Mississippi (Graumann and others 2005). In the South unit of Mississippi where DeSoto National Forest is located, 14 percent of live trees were impacted by the storm (Oswalt and others 2009a). Tree mortality due to Hurricane Katrina may contribute to the creation of early-successional habitat across the Mississippi landscape, and particularly on DeSoto National Forest.

Tree Volume

- The volume of all-live trees on timberland on national forests in Mississippi is about 3 billion cubic feet. The greatest volume occurs in the loblolly-shortleaf forest-type group, with 1.4 billion cubic feet. Longleaf-slash pine forests contain about 621 million cubic feet of volume, while oak-hickory forests contain about 603 million cubic feet of volume.

- Per-acre volume on national forest timberland has increased by 52 percent since 1977, and has increased by 24 percent since 1994, a trend that reflects the maturation of trees on the landscape.

Visitor exit sign on Tombigbee National Forest, Mississippi (photo by Sonja Oswalt, U S Department of Agriculture Forest Service)

- Softwoods comprise a total of 58 percent of live-tree volume on national forest timberland in Mississippi. In 1977, softwoods comprised 66 percent of live-tree volume (fig. 9).

- Sawtimber volume on national forest timberland in Mississippi equaled about 14 billion board feet, with the majority of volume occurring in the loblolly-shortleaf pine forest-type group (6 billion board feet).

- Only 34 percent of sawtimber was categorized as tree grade 1. The remainder of volume occupied mid- to low-grade categories (fig. 10).

- Softwoods accounted for 9.5 billion board feet of sawtimber volume on national forest timberland, statewide.

- Per-acre softwood sawtimber volume on national forest timberland has increased by 29 percent since 1977, while per-acre hardwood sawtimber volume more than doubled in the same time period (fig. 11).

- Longleaf pine volume on national forests did not experience a significant change between 1977 and 2006. Longleaf pine volume on national forests statewide equals 268.8 million cubic feet (fig. 12).

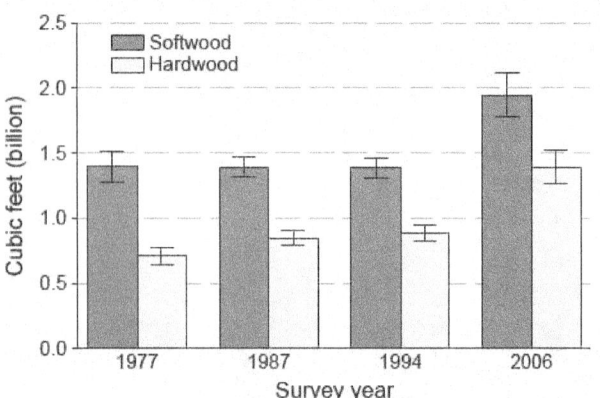

Figure 9—Live-tree volume on national forest timberland (± 1 standard error) by survey year and major species group, Mississippi.

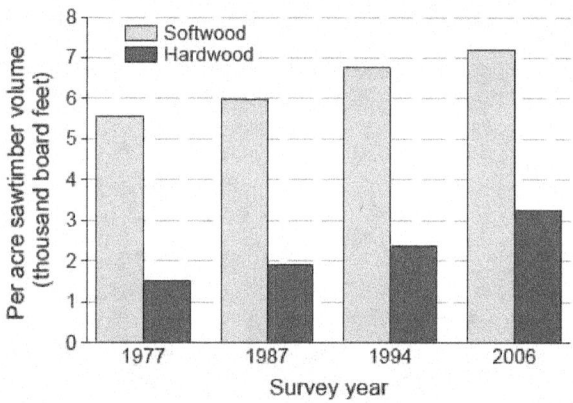

Figure 11—Per-acre sawtimber volume on national forest timberland by survey year and major species group, Mississippi.

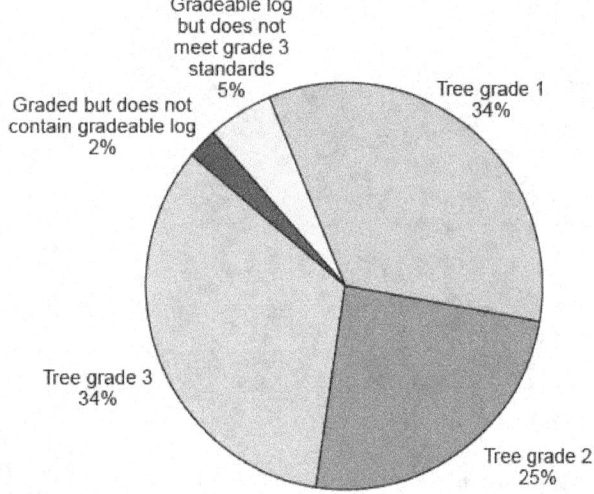

Figure 10—Proportion of sawtimber volume by tree grade on national forest timberland, Mississippi, 2006.

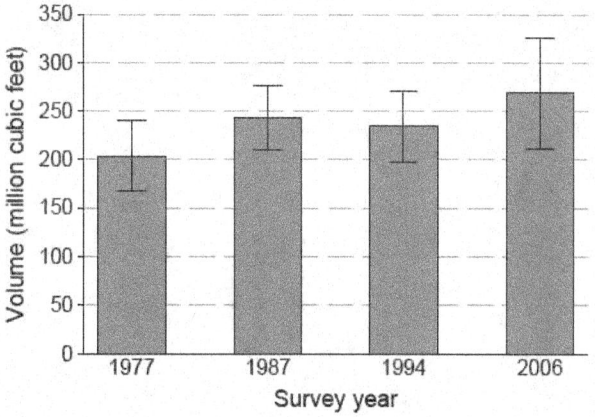

Figure 12—Volume of longleaf pine on national forest timberland (± 1 standard error) by survey year, Mississippi.

Nuttall oak acorn, national forests in Mississippi. (photo by Dean Elsen, U.S. Department of Agriculture Forest Service)

Tree volume is a measure of the amount of wood available in a tree, often for the purposes of determining the economic value of a forest. Loblolly and shortleaf pine trees are very important, economically, to Mississippi and to the national forests in the State. On national forests in Mississippi, most sawtimber volume occupied mid- to low-grade classes, meaning that the wood has defects that reduce its value. However, since national forests are managed for multiresource stewardship, saw-log quality is not necessarily a primary objective of forest management.

Overall, tree volume has increased over the last 3 decades, reflecting the growing and maturing resource on Mississippi's national forests. Most of the volume is composed of softwood trees, though hardwood tree volume has increased significantly.

Longleaf pine is an important ecological species on Mississippi's national forests. Although overall softwood volume has increased on timberland since 1977, longleaf pine volume has not changed significantly. However, small sample sizes may prevent detection of small-scale changes in the resource.

Biomass and Carbon on National Forests in Mississippi

- There were about 80 million tons, or 61 tons per acre (dry weight), of biomass contained in standing live trees and saplings on national forest timberland in Mississippi, an increase of 11 tons per acre since 1994.

- Seventy-two percent of standing live and dead biomass on national forest forest land in Mississippi was in the merchantable bole of the tree, while 15 percent was in branches and foliage, 5 percent was in saplings, and the stump and standing dead trees each made-up 4 percent (fig. 13).

- The biomass contained in live trees on national forest forest land in Mississippi represented 11 percent of total standing live biomass in the State.

- Forty-eight percent of the live-tree biomass was contained in trees > 15 inches d.b.h.

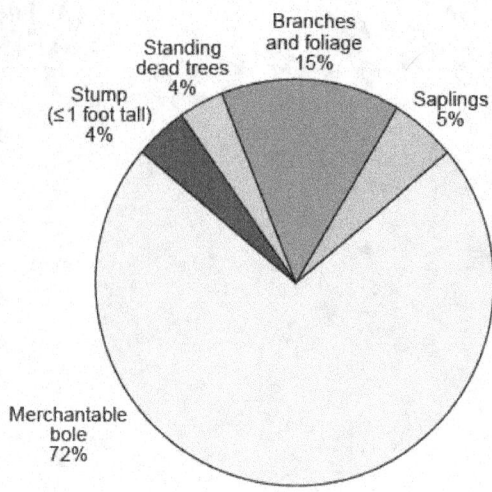

Figure 13—Components of aboveground tree biomass on national forest forest land in Mississippi, 2006.

- Softwoods contributed 52 percent of standing live tree and sapling aboveground biomass, while hardwoods contributed 48 percent.

- Total aboveground and belowground carbon on Mississippi's national forests was estimated at about 88.5 million tons. Forty-six percent of the carbon was in live trees and saplings, 30 percent in soil organic matter, 10 percent in belowground components of live trees and saplings, and 7 percent in litter. The remainder comprises down woody material, aboveground and belowground understory material, and standing dead trees (fig. 14).

Forest biomass, the living material present in a forest system, is a useful measure of tree and forest productivity. More recently, woody biomass has become an industry buzzword related to the domestic energy market and carbon sequestration. Although the national forests in Mississippi represent only 7 percent of the State's forest land, they contain 11 percent of standing live biomass. The preponderance of larger trees on the national forests results in more biomass accumulation than on other forest land in the State. National forests in Mississippi are an important contributor to the State's biomass reserve.

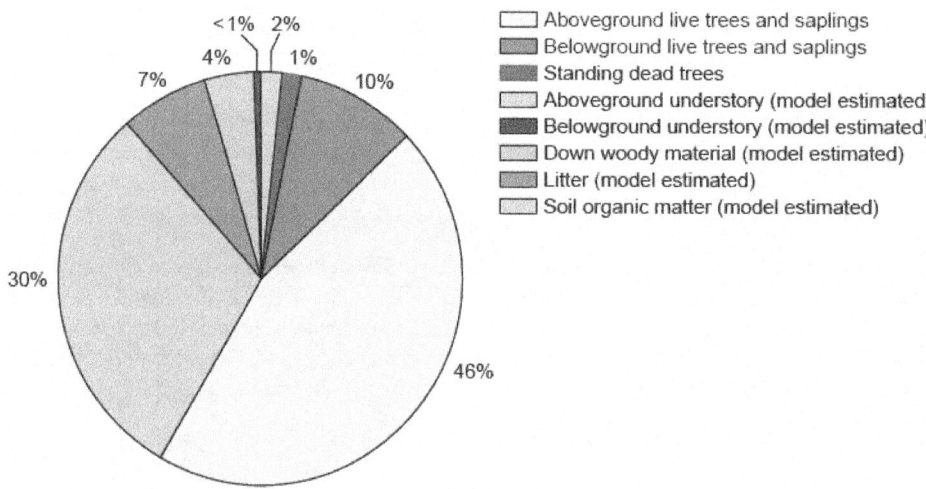

Figure 14—Components of aboveground and belowground carbon on national forest forest land in Mississippi, 2006.

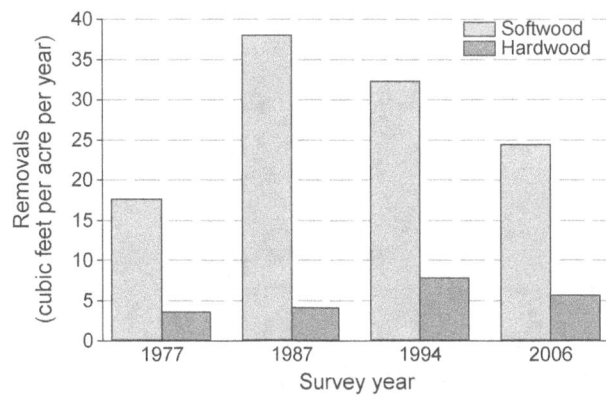

Fishing on DeSoto National Forest in Mississippi, pictured with Smokey Bear. (photo by Ed Moody, U.S. Department of Agriculture Forest Service)

Tree Removals and Growth

- Average annual removals on national forest timberland equaled 39.5 million cubic feet per year, 81 percent of which was softwood removals. Per-acre average annual removals in 2006 were 25 percent lower than in 1994 (fig. 15). Ninety-five percent of average annual removals for the 2006 inventory were due to harvest operations.

- In contrast, average annual net growth was 70.8 million cubic feet. Growth outpaced removals in both softwoods and hardwoods.

- Average annual removals on DeSoto National Forest, at 26 cubic feet per acre per year, are lower than annual removals on non-Federal land in south Mississippi (54 cubic feet per acre per year) and on all timberland statewide (55 cubic feet per acre per year). Removals on DeSoto National Forest are consistent with Mississippi's other national forests, which removed about 33 cubic feet per acre per year.

Figure 15—Average annual per-acre removals (harvest and other) of all-live trees on national forest timberland by survey year, Mississippi.

13

Pine forest in Mississippi. (photo by Christopher Oswalt, U.S. Department of Agriculture Forest Service)

- Average net annual growth on timberland was about 54 cubic feet per acre per year on all national forests in Mississippi, as compared to the statewide average of 71 cubic feet per acre per year. Average net annual growth of live trees was even lower on DeSoto National Forest, with an average of 35 cubic feet per acre per year.

- Net growth on DeSoto National Forest was lower than all other national forests in Mississippi, which averaged net annual growth rates of 70 cubic feet per acre per year— much more similar to the statewide average.

- Average annual net growth on national forest timberland has fluctuated since 1977, but has generally decreased through time (fig. 16). The gradual decline in growth is probably an artifact of aging forests, since growth slows as trees age.

Removals on national forests in Mississippi have declined since the 1980s, a trend that has occurred throughout the southern NFS (Oswalt and others 2009b). Despite the decrease in removals, Mississippi's national forests accounted for the largest proportion (24 percent) of removals from southern national forests during the survey time period (Oswalt and others 2009b).

Tree growth on national forests in Mississippi, while still greater than the amount of wood volume removed, was low compared to the statewide average. Growth slows with age, so the relative older age of trees on the national forests plays a role in the difference in growth rates. Trees on DeSoto National Forest had particularly slow growth rates compared to the statewide average. Since net growth as calculated by

FIA includes mortality, and, as shown in the next section, mortality was high in DeSoto National Forest, it is not surprising that overall growth was comparatively low.

Tree Mortality and Standing Dead Trees

- On average, tree mortality claimed 51.4 million cubic feet of volume per year on national forest timberland in Mississippi. About one-half of that (26 million cubic feet per year) occurred on DeSoto National Forest. FIA averages mortality rates over remeasurement periods. Therefore, it is quite possible that much of the mortality recorded on national forests in the State for the 2006 inventory period was the result of Hurricane Katrina, which primarily affected DeSoto National Forest.

- Per-acre mortality on DeSoto National Forest timberland was five times higher in the 2006 inventory than in the 1994 inventory (fig. 17), and per-acre mortality on other Mississippi national forests was two times higher, most likely because of the impacts of Hurricane Katrina.

- Total mortality on all national forests in Mississippi was < 2 percent of the standing inventory volume.

- There was an average of about eight standing dead trees per acre on national forests in Mississippi. DeSoto National Forest had a larger number of standing dead trees per acre than other national forests, statewide, with an average of >11 per acre. Statewide on all forest land, regardless of ownership, there was an average of six standing dead trees per acre.

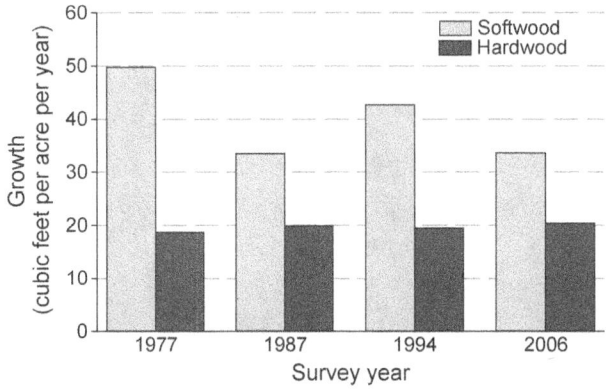

Figure 16—Average annual per-acre growth of all-live trees on national forest timberland by survey year, Mississippi.

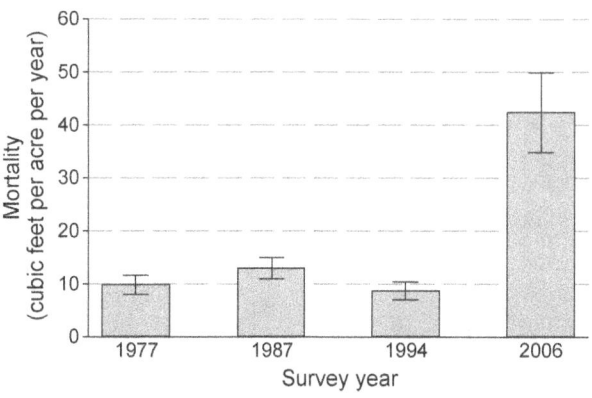

Figure 17—Average annual per-acre mortality on DeSoto National Forest timberland (± 1 standard error) by survey year, Mississippi.

While tree mortality may appear high on national forests in Mississippi, particularly on DeSoto National Forest, it is still relatively low when compared to the total standing inventory. Dead trees are an important component of forest ecosystems. As they decay, they supply necessary nutrients to the soil, serve as substrate for plant and tree seedling growth, and provide shelter for wildlife. Too many dead trees, however, can result in excess fuel accumulation and increased risk of wildfire. A balance is necessary for optimal forest health. In Mississippi, one reason for high mortality on DeSoto National Forest is Hurricane Katrina, which came ashore in fall, 2005. The South FIA unit in Mississippi, where DeSoto National Forest is located, was most heavily impacted by the hurricane.

Additional mortality may occur as trees that were stressed by the hurricane succumb to illness or disease. Gaps in the canopy resulting from dead trees will allow sunlight to reach the forest floor, resulting in regeneration in areas that were impacted by the hurricane.

Acknowledgments

The author thanks field crews operating in Mississippi during the 2006 inventory for their hard work and persistent attention to data quality. Additionally, thanks are due to the reviewers of this manuscript for their invaluable comments.

Literature Cited

Graumann, A.; Houston, T.; Lawrimore, J. [and others]. 2005. Hurricane Katrina: a climatological perspective, preliminary report. Technical Report 2005–01. Washington, DC: U.S. Department of Commerce, National Oceanic and Atmospheric Administration. 27 p.

Holzmueller, E.; Jose, S.; Jenkins, M. [and others]. 2006. Dogwood anthracnose in eastern hardwood forests: what is known and what can be done? Journal of Forestry. 104(1): 21-26.

Little, E.L., Jr. 1979. Checklist of United States trees (native and naturalized). Agric. Handb. 541. Washington, DC: U.S. Department of Agriculture. 375 p.

Oswalt, S.N.; Johnson, T.G.; Coulston, J.W.; Oswalt, C.M. 2009a. Mississippi's forests, 2006. Resour. Bull. SRS–147. Asheville, NC: U.S. Department of Agriculture Forest Service, Southern Research Station. 78 p.

Oswalt, S.N.; Johnson, T.G.; Howell, M.; Bentley, J.W. 2009b. Fluctuations in national forest timber harvest and removals: the southern regional perspective. Resour. Bull. SRS–148. Asheville, NC: U.S. Department of Agriculture Forest Service, Southern Research Station. 30 p.

U.S. Department of Agriculture Forest Service. 2005. Forest inventory and analysis national core field guide. Field data collection for phase 2 plots. Version 3.0. Arlington, VA: U.S. Department of Agriculture Forest Service, Forest Inventory and Analysis Program. Vol. 1. http://fia.fs.fed.us/library/field-guides-methods-proc/docs/2006/core_ver_3-0_10_2005.pdf. [Data accessed: July 7, 2008].

U.S. Department of Agriculture Natural Resources Conservation Service. 2009. The PLANTS database. Baton Rouge, LA: National Plant Data Center. http://plants.usda.gov. [Date accessed unknown].

Standing dead trees in Mississippi. (photo by Christopher Oswalt, U.S. Department of Agriculture Forest Service)

Glossary

Below is a list of commonly used technical terms and their definitions. For additional details, including measurement protocols, see the Southern Research Station's field manual Web site (U.S. Department of Agriculture Forest Service 2005). A discussion of changes to standard terminology since earlier surveys is included in the section on inventory methods.

All-live tree—All living trees. All size classes, all tree classes, and both saw-log and nonsaw-log species are included. See FIA tree species list in the field manual.

Average annual mortality—Average annual volume of trees ≥ 5.0 inches d.b.h. that died from human and natural causes during the intersurvey period, excluding those removed by harvesting, cultural operations, land clearing, or changes in land use.

Average annual net growth—Average annual net change in volume of trees ≥ 5.0 inches d.b h./d.r.c. without taking into account losses from cutting (gross growth minus mortality) during the intersurvey period.

Average annual removals—Average annual volume of trees ≥ 5.0 inches d.b.h. removed from the inventory by harvesting, cultural operations (such as timber-stand improvement), land clearing, or changes in land use during the intersurvey period.

Basal area—The cross sectional area of a tree at breast height or of all the trees in a stand, usually expressed in square feet or square feet per acre.

Biomass—For the Southern region, total aboveground biomass is estimated using allometric equations and is defined as the aboveground weight of wood and bark in live trees ≥ 1.0 inch d.b h./d r.c. from the ground to the tip of the tree, excluding all foliage (leaves, needles, buds, fruit, and limbs <0.5 inch in diameter). Biomass is expressed as oven-dry weight and the units are tons. Note: the weight of wood and bark in limbs <0.5 inch in diameter is included in the biomass of small-diameter trees. Additionally, biomass in the merchantable stem is estimated regionally, where the main and merchantable stems are defined as follows.

Belowground biomass—Coarse roots only.

Gross aboveground biomass—Total tree biomass excluding foliage and roots with no deductions made for rotten, missing, or broken-top cubic-foot cull.

Main stem—The central portion of the tree extending from the ground level to the tip for timber species. For woodland species this includes the portion of the tree from ground level to the tips of all branches of qualifying stems. For timber species trees that fork, the main stem refers to the fork that would yield the most merchantable volume.

Merchantable stem—That portion of the main stem of a timber species tree from a 1-foot stump to a minimum 4-inch top diameter inside or outside bark depending on species. That portion of a woodland species tree from the d.r.c. measurements to the 1.5-inch diameters of all the qualifying stems. Nationally aboveground and belowground biomass is estimated from each tree's sound volume using a component ratio method that is consistently applied in all FIA regions.

Net aboveground biomass—Gross aboveground biomass minus deductions for missing cull, broken-top, and a reduction for a proportion of rotten cull for live or standing dead trees ≥ 5.0 inches d.b.h. (rotten cull will have a factor to reduce specific gravity separately from sound wood). Live and standing dead trees 1.0-4.9 inches only have deductions for broken-top cull. Additional deductions are made for dead trees ≥ 1.0 inch using decay class.

Further, the total net aboveground biomass estimated using the component ratio method is divided into the following components:

Bole—See: Merchantable stem.

Branches—All the branches of a timber species tree excluding the main stem. That portion of all the branches of qualifying stems of woodland species above the 1.5-inch diameter ends.

Top—That portion of the main stem of a timber species tree above the 4-inch top. For woodland species, this component of the biomass is included with branches.

Stump—That portion of timber species below 1-foot to ground level. That portion of woodland species from all the d.r.c. measurements to ground level.

Component of change—References the change in the volume of (live or growing stock) trees 5.0 inches d.b.h. and larger and averaged over the years of the intersurvey period, specifically:

Average annual gross growth—Change in the volume of trees in the absence of cutting and mortality.

Average annual mortality—Volume of trees that died from natural causes.

Average annual net growth—Net change in volume in the absence of removals, and calculated as average annual gross growth minus average annual mortality.

Average annual removals—Volume of trees removed from the inventory by harvesting, cultural operations, (e.g., timber-stand improvement), land clearing, or change in land use and averaged over the years of the intersurvey period.

Diameter at breast height (d.b.h.)—The diameter for tree stem, located at 4.5 feet above the ground (breast height) on the uphill side of a tree. The point of diameter measurement may vary on abnormally formed trees.

Diameter class—A classification of trees based on diameter outside bark, measured at breast height (d.b.h.) above the ground or at root collar (d.r.c.). Note: Diameter classes are commonly in 2-inch increments, beginning with 2-inches. Each class provides a range of values with the class name being the approximate midpoint. For example, the 6-inch class includes trees 5.0 through 6.9 inches d.b.h.

Dry weight—The oven-dry weight of biomass.

Forest land—Land that is at least 10 percent stocked by forest trees of any size, or land formerly having such tree cover, and is not currently developed for a nonforest use. The minimum area for classification as forest land is 1 acre. Roadside, streamside, and shelterbelt strips of timber must have a crown width at least 120 feet wide to qualify as forest land. Unimproved roads and trails, streams and other bodies of water, or natural clearings in forested areas shall be classified as forest, if < 120 feet in width or 1.0 acre in size. Forest land is divided into timberland, reserved forest land, and other forest land (such as woodland).

Forest type—A classification of forest land based upon and named for the tree species that forms the plurality of live-tree stocking. A forest-type classification for a field location indicates the predominant live-tree species cover for the field location; hardwoods and softwoods are first grouped to determine predominant group, and forest type is selected from the predominant group.

Forest-type group—A combination of forest types that share closely associated species or site requirements.

Examples for the Southern Region include the following:

Elm-ash-cottonwood—Forests in which elm, ash, or cottonwood, singly or in combination, constitute a plurality of the stocking. (Common associates include willow, sycamore, beech, and maple.)

Loblolly-shortleaf pine—Forests in which loblolly pine, shortleaf pine, or other southern yellow pines, except longleaf or slash pine, singly or in combination, constitute a plurality of the stocking. (Common associates include oak, hickory, and gum.)

Maple-beech-birch—Forests in which maple, beech, or yellow birch, singly or in combination, constitute a plurality of the stocking. (Common associates include hemlock, elm, basswood, and white pine.)

Oak-gum-cypress—Bottomland forests in which tupelo, blackgum, sweetgum, oaks, or southern cypress, singly or in combination, constitute a plurality of the stocking, except where pines account for 25 to 50 percent of stocking, in which case the stand is classified as oak-pine. (Common associates include cottonwood, willow, ash, elm, hackberry, and maple.)

Oak-hickory—Forests in which upland oaks or hickory, singly or in combination, constitute a plurality of the stocking, except where pines account for 25 to 50 percent, in which case the stand is classified oak-pine. (Common associates include yellow-poplar, elm, maple, and black walnut.)

Oak-pine—Forests in which hardwoods (usually upland oaks) constitute a plurality of the stocking but in which pines account for 25 to 50 percent of the stocking. (Common associates include gum, hickory, and yellow-poplar.)

Hardwoods—Tree species belonging to the botanical divisions Magnoliophyta, Ginkgophyta, Cycadophyta, or Pteridophyta, usually angiospermic, dicotyledonous, broad-leaved and deciduous.

Large-diameter trees—Softwoods ≥9.0 inches d.b.h. and hardwoods ≥11.0 inches d.b.h. These trees were called sawtimber-sized trees in prior surveys. See: Stand-size class.

Litter—Undecomposed or only partially decomposed organic material that can be readily identified (e.g., plant leaves, twigs, etc.).

Medium-diameter tree—Softwood timber species 5.0 to 8.9 inches d.b.h. and hardwood timber species 5.0 to 10.9 inches d.b.h. These trees were called poletimber-sized trees in prior surveys. See: Stand-size class.

Merchantable portion—The portion of the main stem of a timber species tree from a 1-foot stump to a minimum 4-inch top diameter inside or outside bark depending on species. The portion of a woodland species tree from the d.r.c. measurement to the 1.5-inch diameters of all the qualifying stems.

Ownership—A legal entity having control of a parcel or group of parcels of land. An ownership may be an individual; a combination of persons; a legal entity such as corporation, partnership, club, or trust; or a public agency.

Forest industry land—An ownership class of private lands owned by a company or an individual(s) operating a primary wood-processing plant.

National forest land—Federal land that has been legally designated as national forests or purchase units, and other land under the administration of the Forest Service, including experimental areas and Bankhead-Jones Title III land.

Nonindustrial private forest (NIPF) land—Privately owned land excluding forest industry land.

Corporate—Owned by corporations, including incorporated farm ownerships.

Individual—All lands owned by individuals, including farm operators.

Other public—An ownership class that includes all public lands except national forests.

Miscellaneous Federal land—Federal land other than national forests.

State, county, and municipal land—Land owned by States, counties, and local public agencies or municipalities, or land leased to these governmental units for 50 years or more.

Sawtimber-sized trees—Softwood timber species ≥9.0 inches d.b h., and hardwood timber species ≥11.0 inches d.b.h. Now referred to as large-diameter trees.

Seedling—Live trees <1.0 inch d.b.h./d.r.c. that are ≥6 inches in height for softwoods and ≥12 inches in height for hardwoods and >0.5 inch d.b h./d r.c. at ground level for longleaf pine.

Small-diameter trees—Trees 1.0 to 4.9 inches in d.b h./d.r.c. These were called sapling-seedling sized trees in prior surveys. See: Stand-size class.

Softwoods—Tree species belonging to the botanical division Coniferophyta, usually evergreen having needles or scale-like leaves.

Species group—A collection of species used for reporting purposes.

Stand—Vegetation or a group of plants occupying a specific area and sufficiently uniform in species composition, age arrangement, structure, and condition as to be distinguished from the vegetation on adjoining areas.

Stand age—A stand descriptor that indicates the average age of the live dominant and codominant trees in the predominant stand size-class of a condition.

Standing dead tree—A dead tree ≥5.0 inches d.b.h. that has a bole which has an unbroken actual length of at least 4.5 feet, and lean <45 degrees from vertical as measured from the base of the tree to 4.5 feet.

Timberland—Forest land that is producing or capable of producing 20 cubic feet, or more, of wood per acre per year at culmination of mean annual increment (MAI). Timberland excludes reserved forest lands.

Tree—A woody perennial plant, typically large, with a single well-defined stem carrying a more or less definite crown; sometimes defined as attaining a minimum diameter of 3 inches and a minimum height of 15 feet at maturity. For FIA, any plant on the tree list in the current field manual is measured as a tree.

Volume—A measure of the solid content of the tree stem used to measure wood quantity.

Gross board-foot volume—Total board-foot volume of wood inside bark without deductions for total board-foot cull.

Gross cubic-foot volume—Total cubic-foot volume of wood inside bark without deductions for rotten, missing, or broken-top cull.

Net board-foot volume—Gross board-foot volume minus deductions for total board-foot cull.

Net cubic-foot volume—Gross cubic-foot volume minus deductions for rotten, missing, and broken-top cull.

Metric Equivalents

1 acre = 4,046.86 m² or 0.404686 ha
1 cubic foot = 0.028317 m³
1 inch = 2.54 cm or 0.0254 m
Breast height (4.5 feet) = 1.4 m above the ground
1 square foot = 929.03 cm² or 0.0929 m²
1 square foot of basal area per acre = 0.229568 m²/ha
1 cubic foot per acre = 0.0699722 m³/ha
1 pound = 0.454 kg
1 ton = 0.907 MT

Species List

Scientific name[a][b]	Common name	Scientific name[a][b]	Common name
Acer barbatum	Florida maple	*Pinus echinata*	Shortleaf pine
A. negundo	Boxelder	*P. elliottii*	Slash pine
A. rubrum	Red maple	*P. glabra*	Spruce pine
Asimina triloba	Pawpaw	*P. palustris*	Longleaf pine
Carpinus caroliniana	American hornbeam, musclewood	*P. taeda*	Loblolly pine
		P. virginiana	Virginia pine
Carya alba	Mockernut hickory	*Platanus occidentalis*	American sycamore
C. aquatica	Water hickory	*Populus deltoides*	Eastern cottonwood
C. cordiformis	Bitternut hickory	*Prunus americana*	American plum
C. glabra	Pignut hickory	*P. pensylvanica*	Pin cherry
C. laciniosa	Shellbark hickory	*P. serotina*	Black cherry
C. myristiciformis	Nutmeg hickory	*Quercus alba*	White oak
C. ovata	Shagbark hickory	*Q. nuttallii*	Nuttall oak, Texas red oak
Celtis laevigata	Sugarberry	*Q. coccinea*	Scarlet oak
Cercis canadensis	Eastern redbud	*Q. falcata*	Southern red oak
Cornus florida	Flowering dogwood	*Q. incana*	Bluejack oak
Crataegus spp.	Hawthorn spp.	*Q. laevis*	Turkey oak
Diospyros virginiana	Common persimmon	*Q. laurifolia*	Laurel oak
Fagus grandifolia	American beech	*Q. lyrata*	Overcup oak
Fraxinus americana	White ash	*Q. marilandica*	Blackjack oak
F. pennsylvanica	Green ash	*Q. michauxii*	Swamp chestnut oak
Ilex opaca	American holly	*Q. nigra*	Water oak
Juniperus virginiana	Eastern redcedar	*Q. pagoda*	Cherrybark oak
Liquidambar styraciflua	Sweetgum	*Q. palustris*	Pin oak
Liriodendron tulipifera	Yellow-poplar	*Q. phellos*	Willow oak
Magnolia acuminata	Cucumbertree	*Q. rubra*	Northern red oak
M. fraseri	Mountain or Fraser magnolia	*Q. shumardii*	Shumard oak
M. grandiflora	Southern magnolia	*Q. stellata*	Post oak
M. macrophylla	Bigleaf magnolia	*Q. velutina*	Black oak
M. virginiana	Sweetbay	*Robinia pseudoacacia*	Black locust
Malus angustifolia	Southern crab apple	*Sabal palmetto*	Cabbage palmetto
M. coronaria	Sweet crab apple	*Sassafras albidum*	Sassafras
Morus alba	White mulberry	*Taxodium distichum*	Baldcypress
M. rubra	Red mulberry	*Tilia americana*	American basswood
Nyssa aquatica	Water tupelo	*Triadica sebifera*	Chinese tallowtree
N. biflora	Swamp tupelo	*Ulmus alata*	Winged elm
N. sylvatica	Blackgum	*U. americana*	American elm
Ostrya virginiana	Eastern hophornbeam	*U. crassifolia*	Cedar elm
Oxydendrum arboreum	Sourwood	*U. rubra*	Slippery elm
Persea borbonia	Redbay		

[a] USDA Natural Resources Conservation Service (2009).
[b] Little (1979).

Appendix

Index of Tables

Table A.1—Area of national forest by survey unit and land status, Mississippi, 2006

Survey unit	Total area	All forest	Unreserved			Reserved			Nonforest land	Census water
			Total	Timber-land	Un-productive	Total	Productive	Un-productive		
					thousand acres					
Delta	70.6	70.6	70.6	70.6	—	—	—	—	—	—
North	238.0	238.0	238.0	238.0	—	—	—	—	—	—
Central	188.6	188.6	184.2	184.2	—	4.5	4.5	—	—	—
South	608.7	608.7	602.9	602.9	—	5.9	5.9	—	—	—
Southwest	220.6	220.6	220.6	220.6	—	—	—	—	—	—
All units	1,326.5	1,326.5	1,316.1	1,316.1	—	10.3	10.3	—	—	—

Numbers in rows and columns may not sum to totals due to rounding.

— = no sample.

Table A.2—Area of national forest forest land by forest-type group and stand-size class, Mississippi, 2006

Forest-type group	All size classes	Stand-size class			
		Large diameter	Medium diameter	Small diameter	Nonstocked
		thousand acres			
Softwood types					
Longleaf-slash pine	264.0	218.6	32.7	12.7	—
Loblolly-shortleaf pine	471.6	331.0	108.7	31.9	—
Total softwoods	735.6	549.6	141.5	44.6	—
Hardwood types					
Oak-pine	182.8	125.4	33.9	23.5	—
Oak-hickory	258.5	198.2	35.8	24.5	—
Oak-gum-cypress	127.2	96.2	25.0	6.0	—
Elm-ash-cottonwood	11.8	3.0	2.9	5.9	—
Total hardwoods	580.2	422.8	97.6	59.8	—
Nonstocked	10.6	—	—	—	10.6
All groups	1,326.5	972.3	239.1	104.4	10.6

Numbers in rows and columns may not sum to totals due to rounding.

— = no sample.

Table A.3—Area of national forest forest land by forest-type group and stand origin, Mississippi, 2006

Forest-type group	Total	Stand origin	
		Natural stands	Artificial regeneration
	thousand acres		
Softwood types			
Longleaf-slash pine	264.0	225.3	38.7
Loblolly-shortleaf pine	471.6	389.8	81.7
Total softwoods	735.6	615.2	120.5
Hardwood types			
Oak-pine	182.8	167.9	14.9
Oak-hickory	258.5	258.5	—
Oak-gum-cypress	127.2	127.2	—
Elm-ash-cottonwood	11.8	11.8	—
Total hardwoods	580.2	565.3	14.9
Nonstocked	10.6	7.7	2.9
All groups	1,326.5	1,188.2	138.2

Numbers in rows and columns may not sum to totals due to rounding.

— = no sample.

Table A.4—Number of live trees on national forest forest land by major species group and diameter class, Mississippi, 2006

Major species group	All classes	Diameter class														
		1.0–2.9	3.0–4.9	5.0–6.9	7.0–8.9	9.0–10.9	11.0–12.9	13.0–14.9	15.0–16.9	17.0–18.9	19.0–20.9	21.0–24.9	25.0–28.9	29.0–32.9	33.0–36.9	37.0+
		million trees														
Softwoods	179.3	48.2	30.8	33.3	23.7	14.4	8.3	6.5	4.8	3.8	2.4	2.1	0.7	0.2	0.0	0.0
Hardwoods	595.0	388.4	101.3	43.0	23.7	13.6	9.0	5.4	3.8	2.4	1.6	1.1	1.0	0.3	0.1	0.0
All groups	774.2	436.6	132.1	76.3	47.5	28.0	17.3	11.9	8.6	6.2	4.0	3.3	1.7	0.5	0.1	0.0

Numbers in rows and columns may not sum to totals due to rounding.

0.0 = no sample for the cell or a value of > 0.0 but < 0.05.

Table A.5—Net[a] volume of live trees on national forest forest land by forest-type group and stand-size class, Mississippi, 2006

| Forest-type group[b] | All size classes | Stand-size class | | | |
		Large diameter	Medium diameter	Small diameter	Nonstocked
		million cubic feet			
Softwood types					
Longleaf-slash pine	627.7	582.7	40.8	4.2	—
Loblolly-shortleaf pine	1,392.6	1,209.3	172.2	11.1	—
Total softwoods	2,020.3	1,792.0	213.1	15.2	—
Hardwood types					
Oak-pine	409.5	364.0	35.9	9.7	—
Oak-hickory	602.6	541.9	57.9	2.8	—
Oak-gum-cypress	323.1	275.1	42.2	5.7	—
Elm-ash-cottonwood	7.9	6.5	0.8	0.6	—
Total hardwoods	1,343.0	1,187.5	136.8	18.8	—
Nonstocked	0.9	—	—	—	0.9
All groups	3,364.3	2,979.5	349.8	34.0	0.9

Numbers in rows and columns may not sum to totals due to rounding.

— = no sample.

[a] Excludes rotten, missing, and form cull defects volume.

[b] Palm species have been included (species 906 to 915).

Table A.6—Net[a] volume of live trees on national forest forest land by major species group and diameter class, Mississippi, 2006

| Major species group | All classes | Diameter class | | | | | | | | | | | | |
		5.0–6.9	7.0–8.9	9.0–10.9	11.0–12.9	13.0–14.9	15.0–16.9	17.0–18.9	19.0–20.9	21.0–24.9	25.0–28.9	29.0–32.9	33.0–36.9	37.0+
		million cubic feet												
Softwoods	1,962.5	99.2	168.4	192.6	185.3	217.6	234.9	247.7	207.4	245.1	117.7	46.7	0.0	0.0
Hardwoods	1,401.8	115.6	146.3	155.0	167.9	148.8	144.4	122.8	95.4	92.7	129.4	49.6	26.5	7.5
All species	3,364.3	214.8	314.6	347.6	353.2	366.4	379.4	370.5	302.7	337.8	247.0	96.3	26.5	7.5

Numbers in rows and columns may not sum to totals due to rounding.

0.0 = no sample for the cell or a value of > 0.0 but < 0.05.

[a] Excludes rotten, missing, and form cull defects volume.

Table A.7—Net[a] volume of live trees on national forest forest land by forest-type group and stand origin, Mississippi, 2006

| Forest-type group[b] | Total | Stand origin | |
		Natural stands	Artificial regeneration
	million cubic feet		
Softwood types			
Longleaf-slash pine	627.7	568.5	59.2
Loblolly-shortleaf pine	1,392.6	1,251.9	140.7
Total softwoods	2,020.3	1,820.4	199.9
Hardwood types			
Oak-pine	409.5	404.8	4.7
Oak-hickory	602.6	602.6	—
Oak-gum-cypress	323.1	323.1	—
Elm-ash-cottonwood	7.9	7.9	—
Total hardwoods	1,343.0	1,338.4	4.7
Nonstocked	0.9	0.9	—
All groups	3,364.3	3,159.8	204.5

Numbers in rows and columns may not sum to totals due to rounding.

— = no sample.

[a] Excludes rotten, missing, and form cull defects volume.

[b] Palm species have been included (species 906 to 915).

Table A.8—Net[a] volume of sawtimber trees on national forest timberland by major species group and diameter class, Mississippi, 2006

| Major species group | All classes | Diameter class | | | | | | | | | | |
		9.0–10.9	11.0–12.9	13.0–14.9	15.0–16.9	17.0–18.9	19.0–20.9	21.0–24.9	25.0–28.9	29.0–32.9	33.0–36.9	37.0+
		million board feet										
Softwoods	9,454.8	691.3	840.5	1,135.3	1,328.8	1,440.9	1,291.0	1,582.3	801.8	343.0	0.0	0.0
Hardwoods	4,296.4	0.0	481.4	516.8	578.8	560.8	447.2	462.6	741.2	317.6	143.4	46.5
All species	13,751.2	691.3	1,321.8	1,652.1	1,907.7	2,001.7	1,738.2	2,044.9	1,543.0	660.6	143.4	46.5

Numbers in rows and columns may not sum to totals due to rounding.

0.0 = no sample for the cell or a value of > 0.0 but < 0.05.

[a] Excludes rotten, missing, and form cull defects volume.

Table A.9—Aboveground dry weight of live trees on national forest forest land by major species group and diameter class, Mississippi, 2006

Major species group	All classes	Diameter class													
		1.0–2.9	3.0–4.9	5.0–6.9	7.0–8.9	9.0–10.9	11.0–12.9	13.0–14.9	15.0–16.9	17.0–18.9	19.0–20.9	21.0–24.9	25.0–28.9	29.0–32.9	33.0–36.9	37.0+
							thousand tons									
Softwoods	44,947.7	169.0	893.3	2,529.7	3,900.8	4,333.5	4,163.9	4,840.8	5,253.6	5,436.0	4,546.8	5,332.0	2,556.4	992.0	0.0	0.0
Hardwoods	40,780.3	1,734.7	2,535.9	2,891.4	3,510.9	3,773.6	4,146.0	3,784.1	3,746.0	3,228.7	2,766.7	2,739.6	3,562.5	1,277.7	951.2	131.5
All species	85,728.1	1,903.7	3,429.2	5,421.1	7,411.7	8,107.1	8,309.8	8,624.9	8,999.6	8,664.6	7,313.4	8,071.6	6,118.9	2,269.7	951.2	131.5

Numbers in rows and columns may not sum to totals due to rounding.

0.0 = no sample for the cell or a value of > 0.0 but < 0.05.

Table A.10—Merchantable dry weight of live trees on national forest forest land by major species group and diameter class, Mississippi, 2006

Major species group	All classes	Diameter class												
		5.0–6.9	7.0–8.9	9.0–10.9	11.0–12.9	13.0–14.9	15.0–16.9	17.0–18.9	19.0–20.9	21.0–24.9	25.0–28.9	29.0–32.9	33.0–36.9	37.0+
						thousand tons								
Softwoods	37,928.3	1,818.8	3,207.1	3,714.6	3,619.0	4,259.0	4,627.4	4,806.5	4,032.8	4,710.3	2,243.0	889.8	0.0	0.0
Hardwoods	28,553.5	1,958.7	2,681.6	2,968.6	3,333.8	3,040.1	3,014.9	2,620.3	2,134.0	2,143.8	2,819.2	1,066.0	677.0	95.3
All species	66,481.8	3,777.5	5,888.7	6,683.2	6,952.8	7,299.1	7,642.3	7,426.8	6,166.8	6,854.1	5,062.2	1,955.8	677.0	95.3

Numbers in rows and columns may not sum to totals due to rounding.

0.0 = no sample for the cell or a value of > 0.0 but < 0.05.

Table A.11—Total carbon[a] of live trees on national forest forest land by ownership class and land status, Mississippi, 2006

Ownership class	All forest land	Unreserved				Reserved	
		Total	Timberland	Un-productive	Total	Productive	Un-productive
				thousand tons			
U.S. Forest Service national forest	42,864.0	42,488.4	42,488.4	0.0	375.6	375.6	0.0

0.0 = no sample for the cell or a value of > 0.0 but < 0.05.

[a] Estimates of carbon calculated by multiplying aboveground dry tree biomass by 0.5.

Table A.12—Average annual net growth of live trees on national forest timberland by forest-type group and stand-size class, Mississippi, 2006

Forest-type group[a]	All size classes	Large diameter	Medium diameter	Small diameter	Nonstocked
		Stand-size class			
		million cubic feet			
Softwood types					
Longleaf-slash pine	10.7	25.3	3.6	1.8	0.0
Loblolly-shortleaf pine	29.7	15.0	3.2	11.4	0.0
Total softwoods	40.3	20.3	6.8	13.2	0.0
Hardwood types					
Oak-pine	15.8	10.3	1.0	4.5	0.0
Oak-hickory	10.7	4.4	1.2	5.2	0.0
Oak-gum-cypress	3.4	2.8	0.7	-0.1	0.0
Elm-ash-cottonwood	0.5	0.5	0.0	0.0	0.0
Total hardwoods	30.5	18.0	2.9	9.6	0.0
All groups	70.8	38.3	9.7	22.8	0.0

Numbers in rows and columns may not sum to totals due to rounding.

0.0 = no sample for the cell or a value of > 0.0 but < 0.05.

[a] Palm species have been included (species 906 to 915).

Table A.13—Average annual mortality of live trees on national forest timberland by forest-type group and stand-size class, Mississippi, 2006

Forest-type group[a]	All size classes	Large diameter	Medium diameter	Small diameter	Nonstocked
		Stand-size class			
		million cubic feet			
Softwood types					
Longleaf-slash pine	5.8	3.6	1.9	0.4	0.0
Loblolly-shortleaf pine	14.7	13.8	0.3	0.5	0.0
Total softwoods	20.5	17.4	2.2	0.9	0.0
Hardwood types					
Oak-pine	17.0	14.7	1.3	1.1	0.0
Oak-hickory	5.9	3.9	1.3	0.7	0.0
Oak-gum-cypress	7.6	6.8	0.5	0.3	0.0
Elm-ash-cottonwood	0.4	0.4	0.0	0.0	0.0
Total hardwoods	30.9	25.8	3.1	2.0	0.0
All groups	51.4	43.2	5.3	2.9	0.0

Numbers in rows and columns may not sum to totals due to rounding.

0.0 = no sample for the cell or a value of > 0.0 but < 0.05.

[a] Palm species have been included (species 906 to 915).

Table A.14—Average annual removals of live trees on national forest timberland by forest-type group and stand-size class, Mississippi, 2006

| Forest-type group[a] | All size classes | Stand-size class | | | |
		Large diameter	Medium diameter	Small diameter	Nonstocked
		million cubic feet			
Softwood types					
Longleaf-slash pine	7.9	6.5	0.4	0.9	0.0
Loblolly-shortleaf pine	17.9	14.6	2.0	1.3	0.0
Total softwoods	25.8	21.1	2.5	2.3	0.0
Hardwood types					
Oak-pine	9	7.8	0.9	0.4	0.0
Oak-hickory	0.7	0.4	0.3	0.0	0.0
Oak-gum-cypress	3.9	3.9	0.0	0.0	0.0
Elm-ash-cottonwood	0.0	0.0	0.0	0.0	0.0
Total hardwoods	13.7	12.1	1.2	0.4	0.0
All groups	39.5	33.2	3.7	2.6	0.0

Numbers in rows and columns may not sum to totals due to rounding.

0.0 = no sample for the cell or a value of > 0 0 but < 0.05.

[a] Palm species have been included (species 906 to 915).